Bond

Maths

Assessment Papers

9–10 years
Book 2

David Clemson

OXFORD
UNIVERSITY PRESS

OXFORD

UNIVERSITY PRESS

Great Clarendon Street, Oxford, OX2 6DP, United Kingdom

Oxford University Press is a department of the University of Oxford. It furthers the University's objective of excellence in research, scholarship, and education by publishing worldwide. Oxford is a registered trade mark of Oxford University Press in the UK and in certain other countries

First published in 2007 by Nelson Thornes Ltd
This edition published in 2014

British Library Cataloguing in Publication Data
Data available

978-1-4085-2522-7

10 9 8 7 6 5 4 3 2 1

Printed in China

Acknowledgements

Page make-up: OKS Prepress, India
Illustrations: Tech-Set Limited

Before you get started

What is Bond?

This book is part of the Bond Assessment Papers series for maths, which provides **thorough and continuous practice of all the key maths content** from ages five to thirteen. Bond's maths resources are ideal preparation for many different kinds of tests and exams – from SATs to 11+ and other secondary school selection exams.

What does this book cover and how can it be used to prepare for exams?

It covers all the maths that a child of this age would be expected to learn and is fully in line with the National Curriculum for maths and the National Numeracy Strategy. *Maths 9–10 Book 1* and *Book 2* can be used both for general practice and as part of the run up to 11+ exams, Key Stage 2 SATs and other selective exams. One of the key features of Bond Assessment Papers is that each one practises **a wide variety of skills and question types** so that children are always challenged to think – and don't get bored repeating the same question type again and again. We think that variety is the key to effective learning. It helps children 'think on their feet' and cope with the unexpected.

What does the book contain?

- **24 papers** – each one contains 50 questions.
- **Tutorial links throughout** – $\boxed{\text{B} \ 5}$ – this icon appears in the margin next to the questions. It indicates links to the relevant section in *How to do … 11+ Maths*, our invaluable subject guide that offers explanations and practice for all core question types.
- **Scoring devices** – there are score boxes in the margins and a Progress Chart on page 72. The chart is a visual and motivating way for children to see how they are doing. It also turns the score into a percentage that can help decide what to do next.
- **Next Steps Planner** – advice on what to do after finishing the papers can be found on the inside back cover.
- **Answers** – located in an easily-removed central pull-out section.

How can you use this book?

One of the great strengths of Bond Assessment Papers is their flexibility. They can be used at home, in school and by tutors to:

- set **timed formal practice** tests – allow about 30 minutes per paper. Reduce the suggested time limit by five minutes to practise working at speed.
- provide **bite-sized chunks** for regular practice.
- highlight **strengths and weaknesses** in the core skills.

- identify **individual needs**.

- set **homework**.

- follow a **complete 11+ preparation strategy** alongside *The Parents' Guide to the 11+ (see below.)*

It is best to start at the beginning and work through the papers in order. Calculators should not be used.

Remind children to check whether each answer needs a unit of measurement before they start a test. If units of measurement are not included in answers that require them, they will lose marks for those questions. To ensure that children can practise including them in their answers, units of measurement have been omitted after the answer rules for some questions.

If you are using the book as part of a careful run-in to the 11+, we suggest that you also have two other essential Bond resources close at hand:

How to do … 11+ Maths: the subject guide that explains all the question types practised in this book. Use the cross-reference icons to find the relevant sections.

The Parents' Guide to the 11+: the step-by-step guide to the whole 11+ experience. It clearly explains the 11+ process, provides guidance on how to assess children, helps you to set complete action plans for practice and explains how you can use the *Maths 9–10 Book 1* and *Book 2* as part of a strategic run-in to the exam.

See the inside front cover for more details of these books.

What does a score mean and how can it be improved?

It is unfortunately impossible to predict how a child will perform when it comes to the 11+ (or similar) exam if they achieve a certain score on any practice book or paper. Success on the day depends on a host of factors, including the scores of the other children sitting the test. However, we can give some guidance on what a score indicates and how to improve it.

If children colour in the Progress Chart on page 72, this will give an idea of present performance in percentage terms. The Next Steps Planner inside the back cover will help you to decide what to do next to help a child progress. It is always valuable to go over wrong answers with children. If they are having trouble with any particular question type, follow the tutorial links to *How to do … 11+ Maths* for step-by-step explanations and further practice.

Don't forget the website …!

Visit www.bond11plus.co.uk for lots of advice, information and suggestions on everything to do with Bond, the 11+ and helping children to do their best.

Key words

Some special maths words are used in this book. You will find them **in bold** each time they appear in the papers. These words are explained here.

acute angle   an angle that is less than a right angle

factor   the factors of a number are numbers that divide into it, for example 1, 2, 4 and 8 are all factors of 8

improper fraction   a fraction with the numerator bigger than the denominator

lowest term   the simplest you can make a fraction, for example $\frac{4}{10}$ reduced to the lowest term is $\frac{2}{5}$

mean   one kind of average. You find the mean by adding all the scores together and dividing by the number of scores, for example the mean of 1, 3 and 8 is 4

median   one kind of average, the middle number of a set of numbers after being ordered from lowest to highest, for example the median of 1, 3 and 8 is 3

mixed number   a number that contains a whole number and a fraction, for example $5\frac{1}{2}$ is a mixed number

mode   one kind of average. The most common number in a set of numbers, for example the mode of 2, 3, 2, 7, 2 is 2

obtuse angle   an angle that is more than 90° and not more than 180°

polygon   a closed shape with three or more sides

range   the difference between the largest and smallest of a set of numbers, for example the range of 1, 2, 5, 3, 6, 8 is 7

reflex angle   an angle that is bigger than 180° and less than 360°

vertex, vertices   the point where two or more edges or sides in a shape meet

Paper 1

What fraction of the larger shape is the smaller shape?
Work out the **lowest term** fraction for each of these.

1

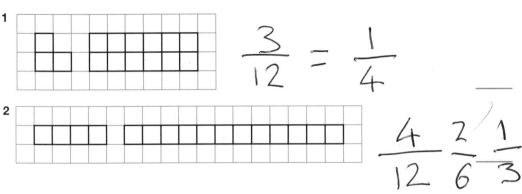

$$\frac{3}{12} = \frac{1}{4}$$

2

$$\frac{4}{12} \quad \frac{2}{6} \quad \frac{1}{3}$$

B 10

2

This is a plan of Jude's ferret cage.

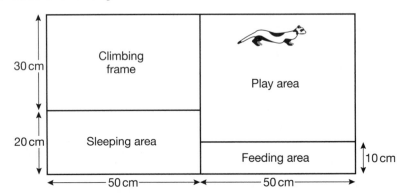

B 12
B 10
B 20

3 What percentage of the cage is used for feeding and playing? _____ %

4 What fraction of the cage is taken up by the sleeping area? _____

5 What fraction of the cage is for feeding? _____

6 What is the area of the cage? _____ cm²

7 What area is covered by the climbing frame? _____ cm²

8 Which has the greater area, the play area or the climbing frame? _____

6

Complete these sequences.

B 7

9–10	26	34	42	___	___
11–12	___	48	39	30	___
13–14	___	36	48	___	72
15–16	36	25	___	___	4	1
17–18	1	2	4	8	___	___

10

Write each of these **mixed numbers** as an **improper fraction**.

B 10

19 $2\frac{1}{2} =$ _____

20 $1\frac{2}{3} =$ _____

21 $1\frac{1}{8} =$ _____

22 $2\frac{3}{4} =$ _____

23 $1\frac{4}{5} =$ _____

24 $2\frac{1}{6} =$ _____

○ 6

What fraction of each shape is grey?

B 10

25 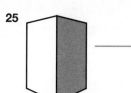 _____

26 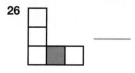 _____

27  _____

28 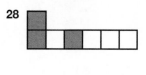

_____

29 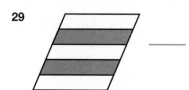 _____

30 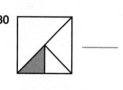 _____

○ 6

Write down the missing numbers.

B 3

31 $206 \times 100 =$ _____

32 $33\,600 \div 100 =$ _____

○ 2

Look at this line graph of temperatures during one week.

B 14

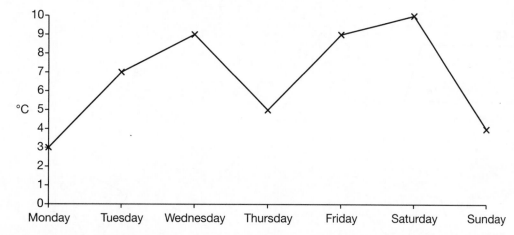

33 On what day was it 5 °C? _____

34 What is the difference between the highest and lowest temperatures? _____°C

35 On which days was the temperature the same? _____ and _____

36 Which was the coldest day? _____

37 Which was the warmest day? _____

○ 5

38 I think of a number. I double it and then double it again.
I then take away 1.
The answer is 15.
What was the starting number? _____

Put a sign in each space so that each question is correct.

39–40 (5 ___ 7) ___ 15 = 20

41–42 (8 ___ 4) ___ 12 = 1

43 Write out in words the biggest number that you can make with these digits.

1   9   7   6   8   3

_____

_____

There are two ropes on a canal narrowboat. The one at the front is 18.6 metres long and the one at the rear is 9.8 metres long.

44 What is the difference in length between the two ropes? _____ m

45 If they were joined end to end how long would they be together? _____ m

46–50 Draw the reflections of these shapes in the line of symmetry.

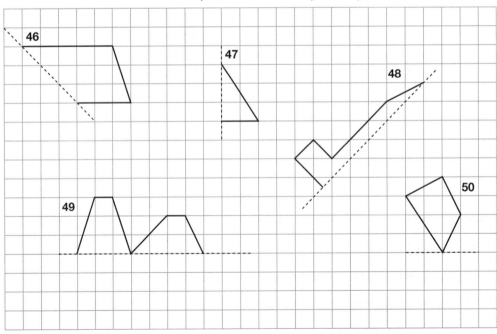

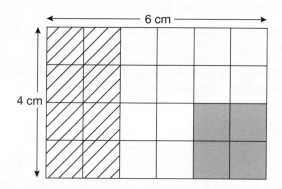

1 What is the area of the whole rectangle? _____ cm²

2 What is the area of the grey part? _____ cm²

3 What is the area of the white part? _____ cm²

Write each of these fractions reduced to its **lowest term**.

4 What fraction of the rectangle is striped? _____

5 What fraction is grey? _____

6 What fraction is white? _____

Look at this map.

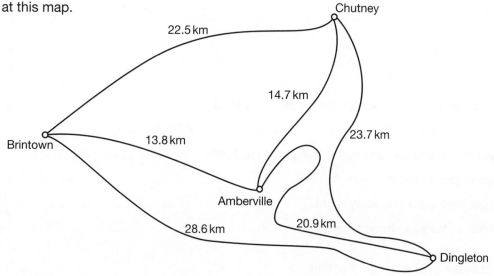

7 How far is it from Brintown to Dingleton via Amberville? _____ km

8 How much further is it from Brintown to Chutney than from Amberville to Dingleton? _____ km

5

9 A delivery van goes from Amberville to Brintown, back to Amberville then on to Chutney and then to Dingleton before going back to Amberville.
How far does the van travel? _____ km

10 How far is it from Brintown to Chutney to Dingleton to Amberville? _____ km

11 How far is the round trip from Dingleton to Brintown to Chutney and back to Dingleton without going through Amberville? _____ km

12 How much further is it from Brintown to Dingleton if you go through Amberville than if you go from Brintown to Dingleton direct? _____ km

13–16 Circle the **obtuse angles**.

a b c

d e f

g h i

Match one of these words to each of the sentences below.

CERTAIN   LIKELY   UNLIKELY   IMPOSSIBLE

17 You will kick a ball so hard that it will go into space. _____

18 You won't get a cold this year. _____

19 It will get dark next Thursday night. _____

20 It will rain in the next three weeks. _____

Write each of these decimals as a fraction.

21 0.3 _____

22 0.09 _____

23 2.37 _____

24 There are 48 children at the Sports Centre. For every 5 boys there are 7 girls. How many boys are there? _____

25 If a lorry uses 4 litres of diesel every 15 km, how many litres will be used in going 300 km? _____

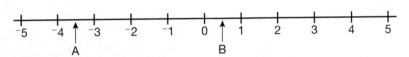

26 What number is arrow A pointing at? _____

27 What number is arrow B pointing at? _____

What number is halfway between:

28 25 and 29? _____

29 36 and 54? _____

30 27 and 49? _____

Underline the correct answer for each question.

31 $4 \div \frac{1}{2} =$		8	2	$2\frac{1}{2}$	$\frac{1}{4}$	1
32 $\frac{1}{6} + \frac{2}{3} =$		$\frac{3}{9}$	$\frac{2}{18}$	$\frac{2}{6}$	$\frac{5}{6}$	$\frac{3}{3}$
33 What is $\frac{2}{3}$ of 21?		$30\frac{1}{3}$	14	$20\frac{1}{3}$	1.4	41
34 How many $\frac{1}{4}$ in 3?		$\frac{1}{12}$	7	13	1.2	12
35 $2.00 - 0.8 =$		1.02	2.08	1.2	12	1.8
36 What is $\frac{1}{3}$ of 18?		3.6	36	9	6	3

Write down the missing numbers.

37 _____ minutes × 6 = 2 hours

38 $4^2 =$ _____

39 25p × _____ = £1.00

40 20p × _____ = £3.00

Multiply each of these numbers by 100.

41 10.75 _____   **42** 31.6 _____   **43** 10.06 _____

44 1.58 _____   **45** 0.43 _____

46–50 Put each of these numbers in the correct box on the Venn diagram.

21, 15, 25, 30, 22

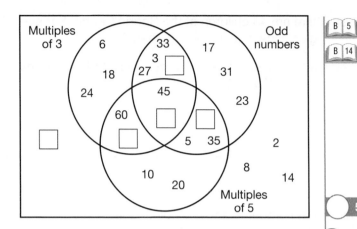

B 5

B 14

5

Paper 3

1 Multiply 32 by 46. _____

B 3

1

Find the total of:

2 £8.57, £21.13 and £4.82.   £ _____

3 £16.58, £27.31 and £8.42.   £ _____

B 2

2

Here is a chart that shows the number of spectators at seven of Dingleton Cricket Club's matches last summer.

4 How many more people watched match 2 than match 3? _____

5 Which match had twice as many spectators as match 3? _____

6 What was the total number of spectators for matches 3, 4 and 5? _____

7 What was the fourth most watched match? _____

8 What was the total number of spectators for matches 1, 2 and 6? _____

9 How many spectators were there altogether at these matches? _____

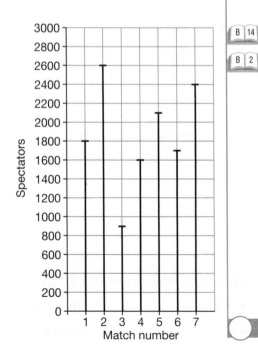

B 14

B 2

6

10 What number, multiplied by itself, gives 49? _____ B 6

11 5 minutes × _____ = half an hour B 27

12 $1\frac{7}{8}$ = _____ eighths B 10

13 $2\frac{2}{3}$ = _____ thirds

14 What is 6 squared? _____ 5

15–17 Write down the numbers that will come out of this machine. B 9

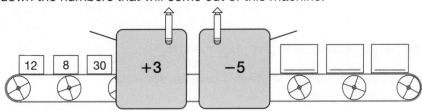

3

Here is a bar-line chart that shows the colours that a spinner landed on when a group of children did a number of spins.

B 14

B 2

B 10

B 12

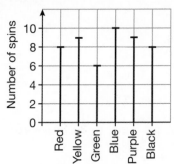 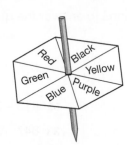

18 How many times did the children spin the spinner altogether? _____

19 How many times did the spinner land on red, yellow or green altogether? _____

20 What is the difference between the total for purple and black and the total for blue and green? _____

21 In its **lowest term**, what fraction of the spins resulted in blue? _____

22 What percentage of the spins were yellow or green? _____ % 5

Answer these questions using the letters a to h.

B 18

B 19

B 24

a 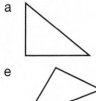   b   c   d

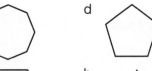

e   f   g   h

23 Which **polygon** is an equilateral triangle? _____

24 Which **polygon** is an octagon? _____

25 Which **polygon** is a right-angled triangle? _____

26 Which **polygon** is a scalene triangle? _____

27 Which **polygon** is an irregular pentagon? _____

28 Which **polygon** has exactly six lines of symmetry? _____

29 Which triangle has only one line of symmetry? _____

30 Divide a 1.2 m rope into 3 equal pieces. How many centimetres is each piece? _____ cm

31 What number, when divided by 9, gives 6 remainder 3? _____

32 Divide 6 litres of squash equally between 4 people. How much squash does each person get? _____ litres

33 What number, when divided by 8, gives 4 remainder 2? _____

Use these two calculations to answer the questions.

$$\begin{array}{r} 847 \\ -\ 486 \\ \hline 361 \end{array} \qquad \begin{array}{r} 438 \\ +\ 375 \\ \hline 813 \end{array}$$

34 $486 + 361 =$ _____   **35** $813 - 375 =$ _____   **36** $847 - 486 =$ _____

37 $813 - 438 =$ _____   **38** $847 - 361 =$ _____

39 There is 1.5 kg of flour in a bag. It takes one-third of a bag to make a loaf. How many bags are needed to make nine loaves? _____

A coach leaves Penrith at 10:37 and reaches Glasgow at 12:05.

40 How long does the journey take? _____ h _____ min

41 $3^2 =$ _____

42 Multiply 9 by itself. _____

43 $\frac{3}{5} + \frac{2}{5} - \frac{1}{5} =$ _____

44 $\frac{8}{10} - \frac{3}{10} + \frac{2}{10} =$ _____

45 $\frac{8}{100} + \frac{91}{100} =$ _____

46 $\frac{36}{100} + \frac{6}{100} - \frac{3}{100} =$ _____

Scale: 1 cm represents 1 m. What does each of these lines represent?

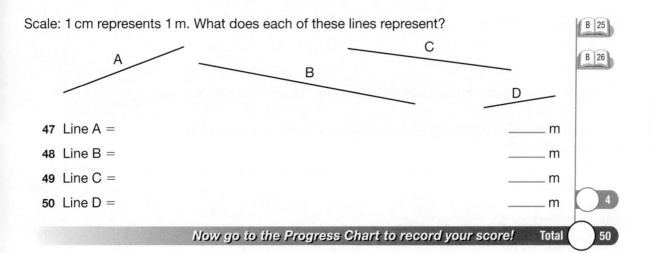

B 25
B 26

47 Line A = _____ m

48 Line B = _____ m

49 Line C = _____ m

50 Line D = _____ m

4

Now go to the Progress Chart to record your score! Total 50

Paper 4

Work out how big the things in this greenhouse are in real life, using a ruler to help you.
Scale: 1 cm represents 1 m.

B 25
B 26
B 20

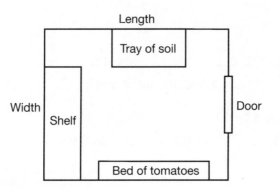

1 How long is the real greenhouse? _____ m

2 How wide is the real greenhouse? _____ m

3–4 How long and wide is the bed of tomatoes in real life?

_____ m long   _____ m wide

5 What is the perimeter of the real shelf? _____ m

6 How wide is the real door? _____ m

7 Which has a bigger perimeter: the bed of tomatoes or the tray of soil?

_____

7

Complete these sequences.

8 36 42 ___ 54 60

9 63 72 81 ___ 99

10 49 ___ 63 70 77

11 What multiplication table contains the same sequence of numbers as in question 8? ___

12 What multiplication table contains the same sequence of numbers as in question 9? ___

13 What multiplication table contains the same sequence of numbers as in question 10? ___

Underline the best approximation for:

14 $\frac{1}{2}$ litre: $\frac{1}{4}$ pint $\frac{1}{3}$ pint $\frac{1}{2}$ pint   1 pint $1\frac{1}{2}$ pints

15 2 miles: 1 km   2 km   3 km   4 km   5 km

16 There are 3 boys for every 2 girls watching the high jump on sports day. If there are 10 girls, how many boys are there? ___

17 James has two stickers in his collection for every sticker that William has. If there are 48 stickers altogether, how many does William have? ___

18 Anish squeezes 5 lemons to make $\frac{1}{2}$ litre of real lemonade. How many lemons does Anish have to squeeze to make 4 litres? ___

19–20 The **factors** of 18 are: 1, 2, 3, ___, ___ and 18.

21 The pairs of **factors** of 10 are: 1 and 10, and 2 and ___ .

Multiply each of these numbers by 10.

22 6.5 ___   **23** 10.3 ___   **24** 0.7 ___   **25** 0.93 ___   **26** 0.08 ___

Look at these shapes.

A   B   C

27 Which shape has two square faces? ___

28 Which shape has only one square face? ___

29 Which shape has the least number of edges? ___

30 Which shape has the most rectangular faces? ___

31 What is the sum of the number of faces and edges for shape B? ___

32 How many **vertices** does shape C have? ___

B 7
B 3
6
B 25
2
B 4
B 13
B 13
B 3
3
B 5
3
B 1
5
B 21
6

33 Multiply 300 by 14. _____

34 What number is 25 less than 71? _____

35 What number is 18 more than 67? _____

Measure these lines with a ruler.

A

B

C

D

36 Line A measures _____ mm.   **37** Line B measures _____ mm.

38 Line C measures _____ mm.   **39** Line D measures _____ mm.

There are 29 586 people in Bigville.

40 To the nearest 1000 this is approximately _____ people.

41 To the nearest 100 this is approximately _____ people.

42 To the nearest 10 this is approximately _____ people.

43 The pairs of **factors** of 15 are: 1 and 15, and 3 and _____ .

44 The pairs of **factors** of 21 are: 1 and 21, and 3 and _____ .

45–46 The pairs of **factors** of 32 are: 1 and 32, 4 and _____, and _____ and 16.

What are these numbers to the nearest 1000?

47 8498 _____   **48** 11 501 _____   **49** 3600 _____

50 Work out how many times you can subtract 9 from 100. _____

Paper 5

Complete these sequences.

B 7

1–2	24	35	___	57	___
3–4	$2\frac{1}{2}$	4	$5\frac{1}{2}$	___	___
5–6	2.95	2.90	___	2.80	___
7–8	88	79	___	61	___	43
9–10	15	___	45	60	75	___
11–12	806	80.6	___	0.806	___

12

A bus driver works five days a week, from 8 o'clock until noon, and from 1.30 p.m. until 5.00 p.m. She has two 15-minute breaks, one in the morning and one in the afternoon.

B2/B3 B4/B27

13 How many hours does she work in a day? _____ hours

14 How many hours does she work in a week? _____ hours

2

Look at this line of black and white counters.

B 7

○ ○ ● ● ● ○ ○ ● ● ● ○ ○ ● ● ●

15 What position in the line is the 8th black counter? _____

16 What colour will the 28th counter be? _____

2

Write the correct sign, $<$, $>$ or $=$, in each space.

A6/B2 B3/B6

17 7×7 _____ $21 + 29$

18 6^2 _____ $26 + 12$

19 $12 + 18 - 2$ _____ 7×4

3

Write 7546 to the nearest:

B 1

20 1000 _____

21 100 _____

22 10 _____

3

B 1

23 What is the biggest whole number that you can make with these digits?

5　0　7　1　9　3 _____

24 Write out the answer to question 23.

_____

_____

2

How would these times appear on a 24-hour clock?

25 Five past 6 in the morning. _____ **26** 12:15 a.m. _____

27 7:30 p.m. _____ **28** One minute to midnight. _____

B 27

4

B 6

29 What number, multiplied by itself, makes 36? _____

30 $7^2 =$ _____

31 What is 8 squared? _____

3

Write the correct sign, $<$, $>$ or $=$, in each space.

32 6 minutes _____ 350 seconds

33 0.75 m _____ 75 cm

34 $12 + 13$ _____ $7 + 8 + 9$

A 6

B 27

B25/B2

3

35 Subtract the product of 8 and 9 from 75. _____

B2/B3

1

36–39 Plot and label the points
A (1,1), B (2,4), C (4,4) and D (4,2).

40 Join up the points. How many lines
of symmetry does this shape have? _____

B 23

B 24

5

Write each of these **improper fractions** as a **mixed number**.

41 $\frac{11}{8}$ _____

42 $\frac{19}{10}$ _____

B 10

2

Two-fifths of the cows on a farm are white. The other 150 are black.

43 How many white cows are there? _____

44 How many cows are there altogether? _____

B 10

2

45 The perimeter of a square is 28 cm. How long is each side? _____ cm

B 20

1

46 Work out how many times you can subtract 23 from 345. _____

B 3

1

Put a number in each space so that each calculation is correct.

47 479 + _____ = 677

48 287 − 149 = _____

49 How many quarters are there in $9\frac{1}{4}$? _____

50 How many days will there be in the first four months of a leap year? _____

Now go to the Progress Chart to record your score!   Total   50

Paper 6

Seventy-two children have each planted a hyacinth bulb to give as a present. 50% of the bulbs produce pink flowers, $\frac{1}{4}$ purple and the rest white. How many are:

1 pink? _____

2 purple? _____

3 white? _____

Some people were asked whether their favourite holiday destinations were beaches, cities or mountains. Their answers are shown in this Venn diagram.

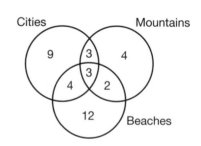

4 How many people were asked? _____

5 How many did not like beaches? _____

6 How many liked both mountains and beaches? _____

7 How many did not like cities? _____

8 How many did not like either mountains or cities? _____

What number is:

9 15 more than 29? _____

10 23 less than 68? _____

16

Calculate the missing angles.

11

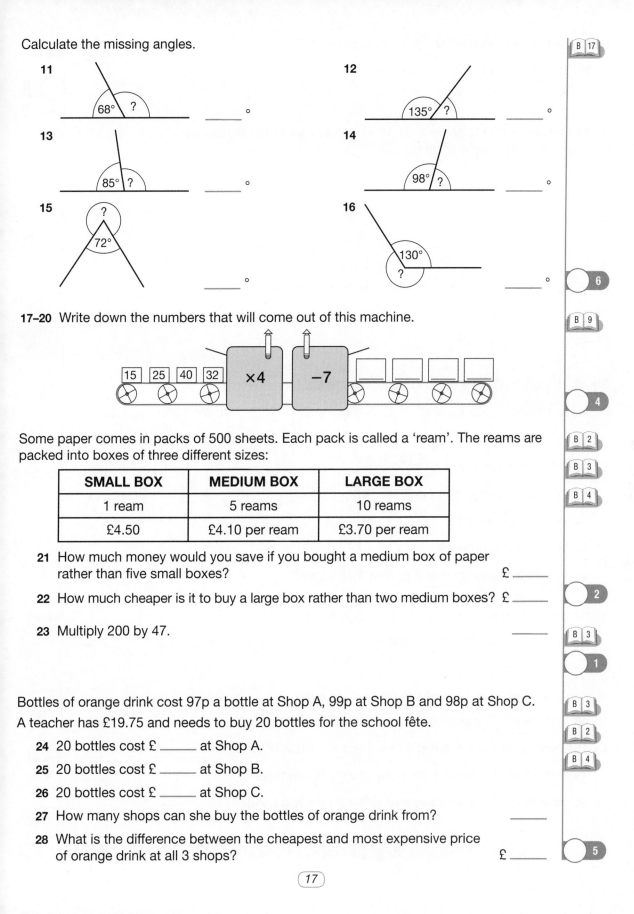

68° ?

_____ °

12

135° ?

_____ °

13

85° ?

_____ °

14

98° ?

_____ °

15

?

72°

_____ °

16

130°

?

_____ °

17–20 Write down the numbers that will come out of this machine.

| 15 | 25 | 40 | 32 | ×4 | −7 |

Some paper comes in packs of 500 sheets. Each pack is called a 'ream'. The reams are packed into boxes of three different sizes:

SMALL BOX	MEDIUM BOX	LARGE BOX
1 ream	5 reams	10 reams
£4.50	£4.10 per ream	£3.70 per ream

21 How much money would you save if you bought a medium box of paper rather than five small boxes? £ _____

22 How much cheaper is it to buy a large box rather than two medium boxes? £ _____

23 Multiply 200 by 47. _____

Bottles of orange drink cost 97p a bottle at Shop A, 99p at Shop B and 98p at Shop C. A teacher has £19.75 and needs to buy 20 bottles for the school fête.

24 20 bottles cost £ _____ at Shop A.

25 20 bottles cost £ _____ at Shop B.

26 20 bottles cost £ _____ at Shop C.

27 How many shops can she buy the bottles of orange drink from? _____

28 What is the difference between the cheapest and most expensive price of orange drink at all 3 shops? £ _____

17

B 17

6

B 9

4

B 2

B 3

B 4

2

B 3

1

B 3

B 2

B 4

5

Underline the calculations that give a remainder of 3.

29–32 $31 \div 2$ $41 \div 4$ $66 \div 9$ $93 \div 10$

       $38 \div 7$ $28 \div 6$ $49 \div 5$ $35 \div 8$

33 The bus is due to arrive at 11:58 a.m. It is running 13 minutes late. At what time will it arrive?   _____

34 Add 24 to 96, then divide your answer by 4.   _____

Put a sign in each space so that each question is correct.

35–36 $(7 \_\_ 8) \_\_ 6 = 9$ **37–38** $(15 \_\_ 5) \_\_ 7 = 10$

39–40 $(7 \_\_ 3) \_\_ 4 = 25$

Six children, A to F, were born on the dates shown.

     A 15/4/97   B 23/6/98   C 2/1/98   D 12/9/98   E 29/12/97   F 2/8/97

41 Who has a birthday in August?   _____

42 Who has a birthday in June?   _____

43 Who has a birthday in April?   _____

44 Who is the oldest?   _____

45 Who is the youngest?   _____

46 Whose birthday is closest to New Year's Day?   _____

There are 64 flowers in the garden. One-eighth of them are red.

47 How many red flowers are there?   _____

On the pond there are 4 moorhens for every 5 ducks.

48 If there are 20 moorhens, how many ducks are there?   _____

On the next pond there are also 4 moorhens for every 5 ducks.

49 If there are 15 ducks, how many moorhens are there?   _____

50 How many birds are there altogether on the two ponds?   _____

Paper 7

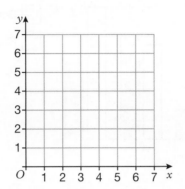

1–6 Plot and label the points A (2,3), B (2,5), C (4,6), D (6,5), E (6,3) and F (4,2).

7 Join up the points. What is the name of this shape? _____

8 How many lines of symmetry does it have? _____

8

These are the results of a mental mathematics test and a spelling test for ten children.

B 15

	Mental mathematics	Spelling
Eric	6	8
Soraya	8	5
Winston	9	8
Ellie	7	5
Francis	10	9
Amy	7	8
Ali	6	7
Daniel	8	4
Patrick	7	8
Amelie	7	6

9 What is the **mode** for mental mathematics? _____

10 What is the **mode** for spelling? _____

11 What is the **range** for mental mathematics? _____

12 What is the **range** for spelling? _____

4

13 Subtract a quarter of 12 from twice 9. _____

B3/B2

1

One of the teachers at Dingleton School asked a group of students where they got their lunch, and drew this bar-line graph of the results:

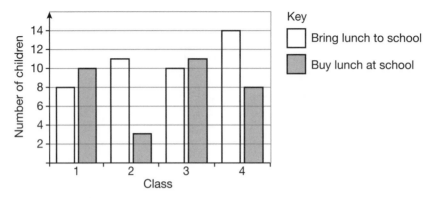

14–21 Complete this table:

Class	Number who bring lunch to school	Number who buy lunch at school
1		
2		
3		
4		

Here is a pie chart that shows what students at Dingleton like best for lunch:

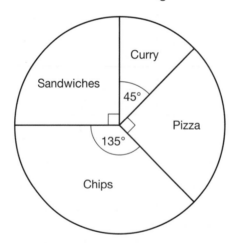

22 What fraction of students like sandwiches best? _____

23 What fraction of students like curry best? _____

24 What percentage of students like pizza best? _____

25 What fraction of students do not like chips best? _____

26 If 100 students like pizza best, how many students are there in the whole school? _____

13

How many halves are there in:

27 14? _____

28 $6\frac{1}{2}$? _____

29 $11\frac{1}{2}$? _____

30 What is the area of the rectangle? _____ cm²

31 What is the area of the black part? _____ cm²

32 What is the area of the white part? _____ cm²

33 Work out how many times you can subtract 0.4 from 2. _____

How many pairs of parallel sides are there in each of these **polygons**?

34 _____

35 _____

36 _____

37 _____

38–40 Write down the missing numbers.

$$7 \text{ remainder } 2$$
$$7) \underline{\hspace{2cm}}$$

$$8 \text{ remainder } \underline{\hspace{1cm}}$$
$$\underline{\hspace{1cm}})74$$

41 My clock gives the time as 8:50 a.m. It is half an hour slow.

What is the real time? _____ a.m.

42 The difference between two numbers is 19. The smaller number is 23.
What is the other? _____

B 10
B 20
3
B 20
3
B3/B11
1
B 19
4
B 3
3
B 27
1
B 2
1

Siva's watch gains 4 minutes every 12 hours. He put his watch right at 9 a.m. on Friday morning.

B 2
B 27

43 What time will it show at 9 p.m. on Friday? _____ : _____ p.m.

44 What time will it show at 9 a.m. on Saturday? _____ : _____ a.m.

45 If he leaves it, what time will the watch show at 9 a.m. on Sunday morning? _____ : _____ a.m.

46 What time will it show at 9 p.m. on Monday? _____ : _____ p.m.

4

Last July the exchange rates for these currencies were:

B 13

£1 = 2.06 Canadian dollars

£1 = 20 Mexican pesos

£1 = 110 Indian rupees

47 How many Canadian dollars can you get for £100? _____

48 How many British pounds can you get for 550 Indian rupees? _____

49 How many Indian rupees can you get for £50? _____

50 How many Mexican pesos can you get for £30? _____

4

Now go to the Progress Chart to record your score!   **Total**   50

Paper 8

Eric and Jamie have 36 football stickers.

B2/B3
B 4

1–2 Jamie has 4 more than Eric. Eric has _____ and Jamie has _____ .

2

3 How many minutes are there between midnight and 2:31 a.m.? _____

B 27

4 How many weeks are there in 196 days? _____

2

Measure each of the angles in this triangle and say whether they are **acute** or **obtuse**.

B 18
B 17

5–6 A _____ ° , _____

7–8 B _____ ° , _____

9–10 C _____ ° , _____

11 What is the sum of all the angles in this triangle? _____ °

12 What is the name of this type of triangle? _____

8

Here is a line graph that shows the outside temperature in February over 24 hours.

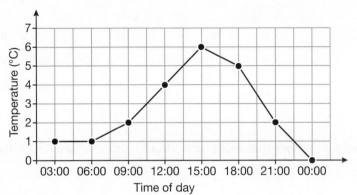

What is the difference in temperature between:

13 9:00 a.m. and midday? _____ °C   **14** 6:00 a.m. and midnight? _____ °C

15 6:00 p.m. and 9:00 p.m.? _____ °C   **16** 9:00 a.m. and 9:00 p.m.? _____ °C

17 The temperature is 8°C. It falls by 11 degrees.
What is the temperature now? _____ °C

18 The temperature is −4°C. It falls by 5 degrees.
What is the temperature now? _____ °C

19 The temperature is −6°C. It rises by 9 degrees.
What is the temperature now? _____ °C

20	8.36	21	2.48	22	1.27
	+ 6.98		+ 3.63		+ 2.58

23 Cyril the snake is 6 cm shorter than Cyrus, his older brother. Cyrus is half the length of a car that is 1.98 m long. How long is Cyril? _____ cm

Here is a pie chart that shows the ways that 48 children get home from school.

24–25 Which two ways are taken by the same number of children?

_____ and _____

26 How many children walk home? _____

27 How many children ride bikes? _____

28 What fraction of children take a bus home? _____

29 What fraction of children go home in a car? _____

I roll a dice three times and end up with a total of 11. What three different numbers might I have rolled?

30 _____, _____ and _____

31 _____, _____ and _____

32 _____, _____ and _____

3

33 What is the smallest number that must be added to 339 to make it exactly divisible by 23? _____

B 5

1

Write each of these decimals as a fraction reduced to its **lowest term**.

B 11

B 10

34 0.07 _____   35 6.5 _____   36 2.9 _____

37 3.25 _____   38 1.75 _____

5

Put a decimal point in each of the following numbers so that the 7 has a value of $\frac{7}{10}$.

B 1

39 1427 _____   40 1742 _____   41 7124 _____

42 1472 _____   43 4217 _____

5

A6/B2

Write the correct sign, $<$, $>$ or $=$, in each space.

B 3

44 $11 - 5 + 4$ ___ $3 + 2 + 7$

B 25

45 5×7 ___ 3×11

B 27

46 $(5 - 2) \times 3$ ___ $(6 + 12) \div 2$

47 0.15 kg ___ 100 g

48 30 m ___ 0.3 km

49 2.5 hours ___ 120 minutes

6

50 What is the perimeter of a rectangle that is 6.4 cm long and 3.2 cm wide?

B 20

_____ cm

1

Now go to the Progress Chart to record your score!   Total   50

Paper 9

1 What will be the colour of the 27th counter in this pattern? _____

2 What will be the colour of the 40th counter in this pattern? _____

3 What will be the colour of the 50th counter? _____

4 Underline the correct answer.

$\frac{1}{4}$ m² =   1000 cm²   1500 cm²   2000 cm²   2500 cm²   3000 cm²

Put a sign in each space so that each question is correct.

5–6 (8 ___ 5) ___ 7 = 6   **7–8** (12 ___ 6) ___ 5 = 11

9–10 (9 ___ 1) ___ 2 = 16   **11–12** (3 ___ 8) ___ 6 = 4

13 Subtract seventy-eight from one thousand and twenty. _____

This is a plan of a garden.

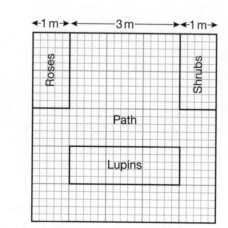

14 What is the area of the rose bed? _____ m²

15 What is the area of the lupin bed? _____ m²

16 What is the area of the path? _____ m²

17 What is the perimeter of the bed of shrubs? _____ m

18 What is the perimeter of the lupin bed? _____ m

B 7   1

B 7   2

B25/B6   1

B2/B3   8

B 2   1

B 20   5

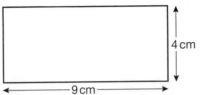

19 What is the area of this rectangle? _____ cm²

20 Underline the dimensions that give the same area as the above rectangle.

5 cm by 5 cm   3 cm by 9 cm   12 cm by 3 cm   8 cm by 3 cm   5 cm by 9 cm

2

21 Wurzitt & Daughters make Super-Wurzitts. Each Super-Wurzitt is 3 m long. On the conveyor belt there is room for 11 Super-Wurzitts with a space of 1 m between each pair of Super-Wurzitts. How long is the conveyor belt?

B2/B3

B 4

_____ m

1

These triangles have been made on a pinboard using elastic bands.
The pins are 1 cm apart.

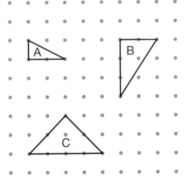

B 18

22 What is the area of triangle A? _____ cm²

23 What is the area of triangle B? _____ cm²

24 What is the area of triangle C? _____ cm²

3

25 Two numbers have a product of 56. One of the numbers is 8.
What is the other number? _____

B 3

1

26 At a fair there was a competition to guess the number of marbles in a jar. There were 400, and the three closest guesses were A: 382, B: 414 and C: 411.
Which was the nearest? _____

B 2

1

The sum of the ages of Annie and Tom is 23.

B2/B4

27 If Tom is 5 years older than Annie, how old is he? _____

28 How old is Annie? _____

2

This is a regular hexagon. Angle b = Angle c and Angle d = Angle e.

B 17

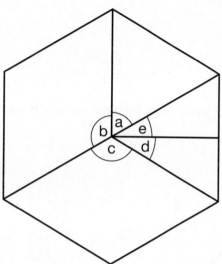

29 Angle a = _____ °

30 Angle c = _____ °

31 Angle e = _____ °

32 Angle b + c = _____ °

4

Calculate the missing angles.

B 17
B 18

33

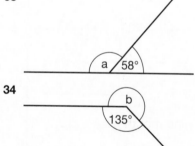

_____ °

34

_____ °

35

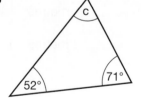

_____ °

3

36 How many days are there in the autumn months of September, October and November?

_____

B 27
1

The perimeter of a rectangle is 36 cm. The rectangle is twice as long as it is wide.

B 20

37 What is its length? _____ cm

2

38 What is its width? _____ cm

These are some measurements of water level from a river, which were taken over a period of nine months.

B 14

B 15

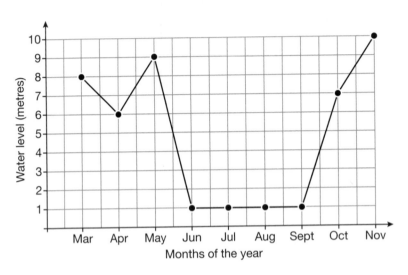

39–41 For which months was the water level higher than the month before? _____ , _____ and _____

42–43 Which months had the lowest water level? _____ to _____

44 Which month was the water level highest? _____

45 The flood level is 10.4 metres. Did the river flood in these nine months? _____

46–47 Between which consecutive months was there the biggest drop in water levels? _____ and _____

48 What is the **range** of water levels over this nine month period? _____ metres

49 What is the **mode** water level over this nine month period? _____ metres

11

50 What is 4567 rounded to the nearest thousand? _____

B 1

1

Now go to the Progress Chart to record your score!   Total   50

Paper 10

Here is a bar chart that shows a robin's visits to a bird table.

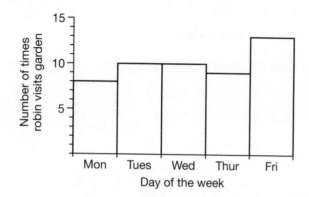

1 On which day did the robin make the most visits? _____

2 What is the total number of visits in the week? _____

3 What is the **mode**? _____

4 What is the **range**? _____

5 What fraction of the week's visits were made on Tuesday and
   Wednesday? _____

I have twice as much money as Anne. She has 46p.

6 How much money do I have? _____ p

7 How much money should I give to Anne if we are to have the same
   amount each? _____ p

8 How much money would we each have then? _____ p

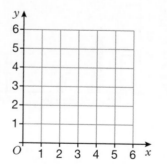

9–12 Plot and label the points A (1,1), B (2,3), C (4,3) and D (3,1). Join up the points.

13 How many **acute angles** does this shape have? _____

14 Translate this shape 2 units up and draw its new position.

There are 320 parrots in the jungle. 20% are red, $\frac{1}{4}$ are blue, 5% are green, $\frac{1}{8}$ are yellow and 10% are purple.

15–16 There are _____ yellow parrots and _____ red ones.

17–18 There are _____ green parrots and _____ purple ones.

19 How many blue parrots are there? _____

20 How many other parrots are there in the jungle? _____

21 What is the smallest whole number that you can make with these digits?

8   4   2   7   3   6

_____

22 Write out the answer to question 21 in words.

_____

_____

Place these numbers in order from largest to smallest.

23–27 4.11   4.101   4.111   4.01   4.1   _____, _____, _____, _____, _____

28 One carpet tile is $\frac{3}{4}$ metre long. How many carpet tiles could be fitted into a room 9 metres long? _____

29 The train left Bigville at 2:35 p.m. and got to Smalltown at 5:25 p.m. How long did the journey take? _____ h _____ min

30 Tamsin bought three toys that all cost the same. She paid with a £10 note and got £1.03 change. How much did each toy cost? £ _____

31 How much is left from £5 if Chris buys 4 pens at 85p each? £ _____

Here is a bar chart that shows the number of days children were absent from school because they were sick.

Key
☐ Term 1
▨ Term 2
■ Term 3

32 Who was sick the most in Term 1? _____

33 Who was sick the least in Term 3? _____

34 Who was sick the most in total? _____

35 Who was sick on two days over the three terms? _____

36 In what term were the most days taken off sick? _____

A flight took off at 8:15 p.m. and landed at 7:45 a.m.

37 How long did the journey take? _____ h _____ min

B 17
1

How many quarters are there in these numbers?

38–41 $3\frac{1}{2}$ = _____ $1\frac{1}{4}$ = _____ $4\frac{1}{4}$ = _____ $2\frac{1}{2}$ = _____

B 10

How many halves are there in these numbers?

42–45 11 = _____ $7\frac{1}{2}$ = _____ $9\frac{1}{2}$ = _____ 15 = _____

B 10
8

30 people have registered for football training. Today nine times as many turned up as did not.

B 13

46 How many turned up? _____

B 3

47 How many were absent? _____

2

48 431
× 4
_____

49 156
× 20
_____

50 7.98
× 6
_____

B 3
3

Now go to the Progress Chart to record your score! **Total** 50

Paper 11

Four-ninths of the cars in the car park are estates. The rest are saloons. There are 27 cars altogether.

B 10

1 How many estate cars are there? _____

2 How many saloon cars are there? _____

2

Here are some thermometers that show the temperatures at midday over four days in summer.

B 14

3 What was Monday's temperature? _____ °C

4 What was Saturday's temperature? _____ °C

5 What was Sunday's temperature? _____ °C

6 What was Friday's temperature? _____ °C

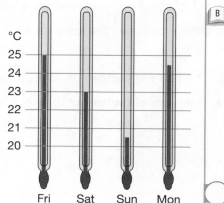

4

7 Write out 17 451 in words.

_____

8   9.45   **9**   15.16   **10**   644
      − 3.68   + 17.47   ×   6.2
      _____   _____   _____

Put a decimal point in each of the following numbers so that the 6 has a value of 6 units.

11 16739 _____   **12** 93617 _____

13 67139 _____   **14** 91367 _____

Write down the missing numbers.

15 $6 \times 4 \times$ _____ = 240   **16** $2 \times 9 \times$ _____ = 90

17 $8 \times 2 \times$ _____ = 48   **18** $5 \times 7 \times$ _____ = 280

19 _____ minutes $\times$ 12 = 2 hours

Mont Blanc in the Alps is 15 771 feet (4807 m) high. Give its approximate height:

20 to the nearest 1000 m.   _____ m

21 to the nearest 100 m.   _____ m

22 to the nearest 10 m.   _____ m

Jeff bought 100 g of chocolate for £1.40, Karin bought 250 g of chocolate for £3.40 and Omar bought $\frac{1}{2}$ a kilo of chocolate for £6.45.

23 What would a kilogram of Jeff's chocolate cost?   £ _____

24 What would a kilogram of Karin's chocolate cost?   £ _____

25 Who would pay the most for a kilogram of chocolate?   _____

26 Who would pay the least for a kilogram of chocolate?   _____

27–28 The pairs of **factors** of 26 are: 1 and 26, and _____ and _____ .

29–34 The pairs of **factors** of 30 are: 1 and 30, _____ and _____, _____ and _____,

and _____ and _____ .

35 What is $7^2 - 5^2$?   _____

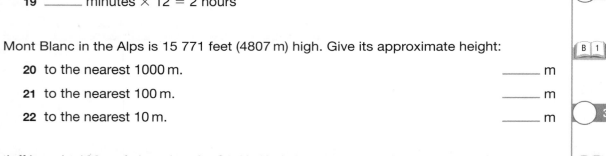

Carly needs to buy a class a set of 30 rulers and she has exactly £33.
A shatterproof ruler costs £1.09 at Shop A, £1.15 at Shop B and £1.12 at Shop C.

B3/B2

36 30 rulers cost £ _____ at Shop A.

37 30 rulers cost £ _____ at Shop B.

38 30 rulers cost £ _____ at Shop C.

39 Which shop can Carly buy the 30 rulers from?   Shop _____

40 How much change will Carly get?   _____ p

5

41–46 Circle the **polygons** that have a true axis of symmetry.

B 19

B 24

a   b   c   d

e   f   g   h

6

Complete these sequences.

B 7

47–48 2.5   2.75   3   _____   _____

49–50 16   8   4   2   _____   _____

4

Now go to the Progress Chart to record your score!   Total   50

Paper 12

A class of children did some research on roses in the local park. Here is a Venn diagram of the results.

B 14

B 2

1 How many roses did the group examine?   _____

2 How many white roses were there?   _____

3 How many scented roses were there?   _____

4 How many white roses were scented?   _____

5 How many roses did they find that had no scent?   _____

6 How many roses were not white and not scented?   _____

White roses 7   2   Scented roses 9

3

6

The coach leaves Exeter for Reading at 06:53. The journey takes 2 hours 34 minutes.

7 What time does the coach arrive at Reading? _____

B 27
1

Multiply each of these numbers by 100.

8 0.36 _____

9 0.83 _____

10 0.0072 _____

B 1
3

This is a plan of Mr Macgregor's garden.

Scale: 1 cm represents 3 m.

B 20
B 3
B 6

Flowers	Vegetables
Path	

$\longleftarrow$—21 m—$\longrightarrow$

11 What area of the garden is for vegetables? _____ m²

12 What is the area of the path? _____ m²

13 Mr Macgregor is going to cover his vegetable patch with paving. How many paving stones will he need if they are each 1 m $\times$ 1 m? _____

14 He decides to cover the flower bed with paving stones too. How many more paving stones will he need? _____

15 If Mr Macgregor decides to cover the whole garden with his new paving stones, how many more does he need? _____

5

There are 32 fish in the pond in Gary's garden. For every 3 carp there are 5 goldfish.

16 How many goldfish are there? _____

17 How many fewer carp are there? _____

B 13
2

Write each of these fractions as a decimal.

18 $\frac{43}{100}$ _____

19 $\frac{13}{100}$ _____

20 $\frac{60}{100}$ _____

21 $\frac{7}{100}$ _____

B 10
B 11
4

The sum of two numbers is 39. The difference between them is 7.

B 2

22 What is the larger number? _____

23 What is the smaller number? _____

2

The volcanic mountain Teide on the island of Tenerife is 12 188 feet (3715 m) high. Give its approximate height:

B 1

24 to the nearest 1000 feet. _____ feet

25 to the nearest 100 feet. _____ feet

26 to the nearest 10 feet. _____ feet

3

Here is a set of numbers: 28, 36, 31, 39, 33, 37.

B 5
B 3

27 Which of these can be divided exactly by 3 and 4? _____

28 Which of these has a remainder of 4 when divided by 6? _____

29 Which of these has a remainder of 3 when divided by 9? _____

30 Which of these has a remainder of 2 when divided by 7? _____

31 Which of these has a remainder of 1 when divided by 8? _____

5

32–35 Write down the missing numbers.

$$9\overline{)}\quad 6 \text{ remainder } 2$$

_____

$$6\overline{)}\quad 8 \text{ remainder } 5$$

_____

$$8\overline{)59}\quad \underline{} \text{ remainder } 3$$

$$7\overline{)47}\quad \underline{} \text{ remainder } 5$$

B 3
4

36–39 Draw the reflections of these shapes in the mirror lines.

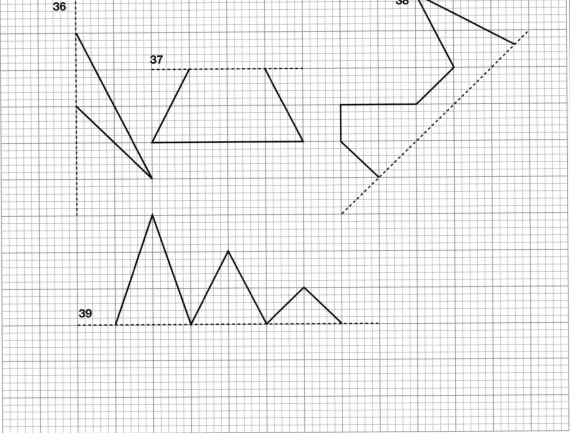

36   37   38   39

4

250 buns are to be packed into tins. Each tin holds 58 buns.

40 How many tins are required?   _____

1

Write each of these fractions as a percentage.

41 $\frac{3}{10}$ _____ %   **42** $\frac{10}{25}$ _____%   **43** $\frac{12}{20}$ _____ %

44 $\frac{30}{50}$ _____ %   **45** $\frac{15}{50}$ _____ %   **46** $\frac{35}{50}$ _____ %

6

Write down the numbers that will come out of this machine.

47–50

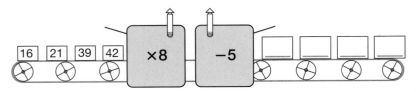

16   21   39   42   ×8   −5

4

Now go to the Progress Chart to record your score!   **Total**   50

Paper 13

Calculate the missing angles.

1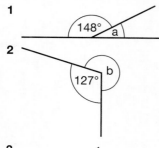

2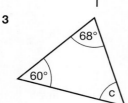

_____°

_____°

3

_____°

Use this calculation to answer the questions.

$$
\begin{array}{r}
84 \\
+\ 68 \\
\hline
152 \\
\hline
\end{array}
$$

4
$$
\begin{array}{r}
184 \\
+\ 168 \\
\hline
\end{array}
$$

5
$$
\begin{array}{r}
384 \\
+\ 68 \\
\hline
\end{array}
$$

6
$$
\begin{array}{r}
484 \\
+\ 168 \\
\hline
\end{array}
$$

Write down the missing numbers.

7 $3 \times 9 \times$ _____ $= 135$

8 $4 \times 10 \times$ _____ $= 200$

9 $3 \times 2.1 =$ _____

10 $5 \times 0.06 =$ _____

11 Write twenty thousand and fifteen in figures. _____

Here is a list of measurements. For each question, choose the correct answer from this list.

24 cm　24 cm²　24 m　30 cm　30 cm²　30 m²　36 cm²　36 m　36 m²

12 What is the area of an envelope that is 12 cm long and 3 cm wide? _____

13 What is the perimeter of the envelope? _____

14 What is the perimeter of a square room that has sides of 6 m? _____

15 What is the area of the square room? _____

B 17

B 2

3

3

B 3

4

B 1

1

B 20

4

Rod sells sandwiches from Monday to Thursday. He sells 53 every day.

16 How many sandwiches does Rod sell in one week? _____

17 If it takes Rod 65 minutes to sell 53 sandwiches, how much
time does he spend selling them each week? _____ h _____ min

Write down all the numbers between 25 and 50 that are multiples of:

18–21 6 _____ , _____ , _____ and _____

22–24 9 _____ , _____ and _____

Write down the missing numbers.

25 250 m $\times$ 12 = _____ km

26 25 cm $\times$ _____ = 1 metre

27 25 ml $\times$ 20 = _____ litre

Here is a pictogram that shows the number of birds that visited the school bird table in one week.

Key: stands for 2 birds

28 How many blackbirds visited the bird table? _____

29 What fraction of the birds were sparrows? _____

30 How many blue tits visited the bird table? _____

31 How many more chaffinches visited than pigeons? _____

32 How many birds visited altogether? _____

33 The kitchen clock gains two minutes every day. If I put it right at noon on
Sunday what time will it show at noon the following Friday? _____

34 What is the size of the smaller angle between the arrow and S? _____ °

35 What is the size of the larger angle between the arrow and S? _____ °

36 What is the size of the smaller angle between the arrow and N? _____ °

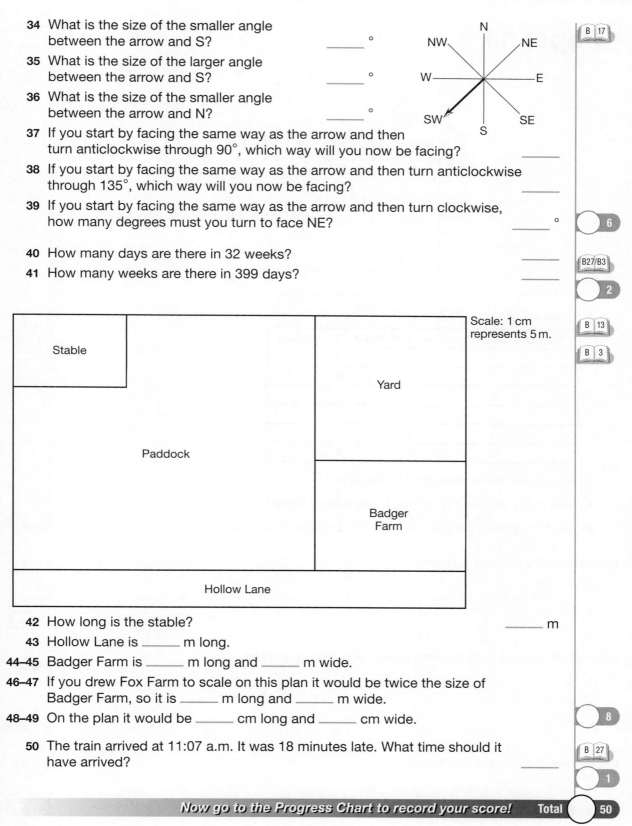

37 If you start by facing the same way as the arrow and then turn anticlockwise through 90°, which way will you now be facing? _____

38 If you start by facing the same way as the arrow and then turn anticlockwise through 135°, which way will you now be facing? _____

39 If you start by facing the same way as the arrow and then turn clockwise, how many degrees must you turn to face NE? _____ °

40 How many days are there in 32 weeks? _____

41 How many weeks are there in 399 days? _____

Scale: 1 cm represents 5 m.

42 How long is the stable? _____ m

43 Hollow Lane is _____ m long.

44–45 Badger Farm is _____ m long and _____ m wide.

46–47 If you drew Fox Farm to scale on this plan it would be twice the size of Badger Farm, so it is _____ m long and _____ m wide.

48–49 On the plan it would be _____ cm long and _____ cm wide.

50 The train arrived at 11:07 a.m. It was 18 minutes late. What time should it have arrived? _____

B 17

6

B27/B3

2

B 13

B 3

8

B 27

1

Now go to the Progress Chart to record your score! **Total** 50

Paper 14

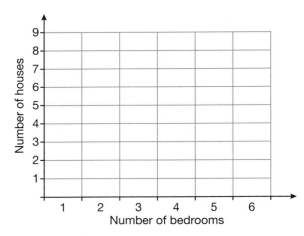

1–6 Draw the bars on the chart above using the numbers from the table.

Number of bedrooms	Number of houses
1	4
2	6
3	8
4	6
5	2
6	1

7 What is the **mode** number of bedrooms? _____

8 How many houses have three bedrooms or more? _____

9 What fraction of the houses have two bedrooms or fewer? _____

Write down the missing numbers.

10 $4 - 2\frac{7}{10} =$ _____

11 $7 - 4\frac{2}{7} =$ _____

Write each of these **improper fractions** as a **mixed number**.

12 $\frac{17}{10}$ _____

13 $\frac{9}{5}$ _____

14 $\frac{7}{3}$ _____

Write down the missing numbers.

15 $8396 = 8000 + 300 +$ _____ $+ 6$

16 $4173 = 4000 + 100 + 70 +$ _____

Write down the missing numbers.

B2/B3

17 $(9 \times 3) +$ _____ $= 36$

18 $4 \times 5 \times$ _____ $= 60$

19 $7 \times$ _____ $= 20 + 15$

20 $8 + 5 +$ _____ $= 16$

21–26 The pairs of **factors** of 32 are: ____ and ____ , ____ and ____ , and ____ and ____ .

27 October had 11 sunny days. Half the remaining days were rainy. How many rainy days were there? _____

28 Subtract twice 7 from half 58. _____

Place these numbers in ascending order.

29–33 52 971   297 135   79 315   325 179   95 713.2

_____   _____   _____   _____   _____

Write down the number of halves in these numbers.

34 $4\frac{1}{2}$ _____

35 6 _____

36 $8\frac{1}{2}$ _____

37 5 _____

38 $9\frac{1}{2}$ _____

39 $11\frac{1}{2}$ _____

40 Work out how many times you can subtract 11 from 231. _____

41 A square has sides that are 0.9 m long. What is the distance all the way round the square? _____ m

The sum of two numbers is 43.

42 If one number is 29, what is the other number? _____

You need to add three parts of water to every one part of lemon squash.

43 How many litres of drink can be made with a litre of squash? _____

44 What is the smallest number that can be divided by 9 and 6 without any remainder? _____

A tennis match lasted 2 hours and 15 minutes and ended at 14:10.

45 What time did the tennis match start? _____

46 The players had a break 1 hour and 5 minutes before the end of the game.
What was the time? _____

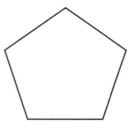

47 Is this **polygon** regular or irregular? _____

48 Draw all of the diagonals in the shape.

49 What is the shape you have made at the centre? _____

Divide a ribbon that is 3.52 m long into 8 equal pieces.

50 How long is each piece? _____ cm

Now go to the Progress Chart to record your score!   **Total**   50

Paper 15

Write each of these fractions as a percentage.

1 $\frac{10}{20} =$ _____ %   **2** $\frac{10}{50} =$ _____ %   **3** $\frac{12}{20} =$ _____ %

4 $\frac{17}{20} =$ _____ %   **5** $\frac{10}{25} =$ _____ %   **6** $\frac{33}{50} =$ _____ %

Shape
A

Shape
B

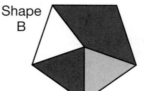

7 How many lines of symmetry does Shape A have? _____

8 What fraction of Shape B is grey? _____

9 What fraction of Shape B is black? _____

10 What is this fraction as a percentage? _____ %

11 What percentage of Shape B is not grey or black? _____ %

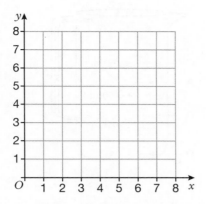

B 23
B 24

12–14 Plot and label the points A (1,1), B (5,1) and C (3,7). Join up the points.

15 What is the name of this sort of triangle? _____

16 How many lines of symmetry does it have? _____

5

Some of these nets make a cube. Write 'Yes' next to those that do, and 'No' next to those that don't.

B 21

17

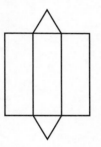 _____

18

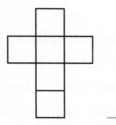 _____

19

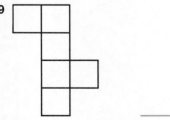 _____

20

 _____

21

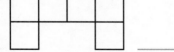 _____

5

Write 5636 to the nearest:

B 1

22 1000 _____

23 100 _____

24 10 _____

3

Look at this 1-litre jug.

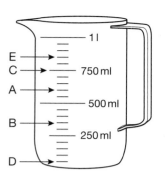

25 A to E measures   _____ ml

26 B to A measures   _____ ml

27 D to C measures   _____ ml

28 B to E measures   _____ ml

29 D to B measures   _____ ml

30 A to C measures   _____ ml   **6**

31 What is the smallest whole number that you can make with these digits?

     8   7   8   5   _____

32 What is the largest whole number that you can make with these digits?

     1   3   5   2   _____

33 Which of the answers to questions 31 and 32 is smaller?   _____

34 What is the difference between the answers to questions 31 and 32?   _____

4

Write each of these **mixed numbers** as an **improper fraction**.

35 $3\frac{1}{2}$ _____   **36** $4\frac{1}{5}$ _____   **37** $2\frac{2}{3}$ _____

38 $1\frac{4}{7}$ _____   **39** $5\frac{2}{5}$ _____

5

40 Which of the following numbers has the highest value?

    $1\frac{1}{2}$ $1\frac{3}{4}$ $1\frac{2}{5}$ $1\frac{3}{8}$ $1\frac{3}{5}$ _____

1

41–42 Write down the missing fractions.

    $\frac{1}{3}$ $\frac{2}{6}$ $\frac{3}{9}$ _____ $\frac{5}{15}$ _____

2

What number needs to be added to or subtracted from:

    43 915 to turn it into 9915?   _____

    44 5893 to turn it into 5693?   _____

2

Draw the lines of symmetry.

45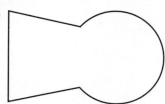

46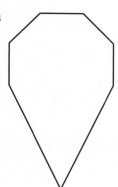

47 276 + 99 =

48 834 + 99 =

49 386 + 99 =

50 503 + 99 =

Now go to the Progress Chart to record your score!   Total   50

Paper 16

	Jane	Jack	Stephen	Melanie
Maths	73	82	77	85
Science	79	80	69	79
English	86	77	84	79
History	71	72	79	78
TOTALS				

1–4 Write each child's total in the table.

5 Who had the highest mark in any one exam?

6 Who had the lowest mark in any one exam?

7 What was the **range** of Jack's marks?

8 Who had the lowest **range** of marks?

9 What was the **mode** mark for all subjects?

10 In what subject was the highest total of marks gained?

11 In what subject was the lowest total of marks gained?

B 24

2

B 2

4

B 14

B 2

B 15

11

Multiply these numbers by 100.

12 2.45 _____

13 0.205 _____

14 24.5 _____

15 204.5 _____

16 2450 _____

Here is a bar chart that shows how many daily newspapers were sold by a newsagent over six days.

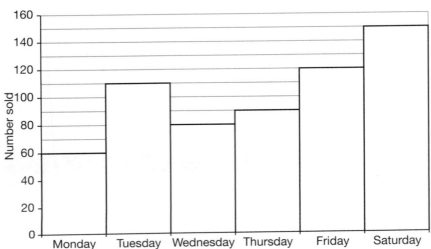

17 How many were sold on Tuesday? _____

18 How many were sold on Saturday? _____

19 On which day were the most newspapers sold? _____

20 How many more were sold on Friday than on Wednesday? _____

21–22 On which two days did the sales add up to Saturday's total? _____ and _____

23 How many newspapers were sold over the six days? _____

Write 'True' next to the statements that are true and 'False' next to those that are false.

24 $(155 \times 10) > (15 \times 100)$ _____

25 $(3.75 \times 100) < (37 \times 10)$ _____

26 $(35.5 \times 10) < (3.55 \times 100)$ _____

27 $(16.58 \times 10) > (1.685 \times 100)$ _____

28 What is the area of a carpet that measures 4.5 m × 3.5 m? _____ m²

29 A rectangle has an area of 27 cm². Its width is 4 cm. What is its length?

_____ cm

30 Add five hundred and twenty-nine to three thousand, eight hundred and thirty-two. Write the answer in figures.

_____

B1/B2
1

I ate half of my sweets and had 28 left.

31 How many did I have at the start?

_____

B 3
1

32 What is the perimeter of a rectangle 5.7 cm long and 4.4 cm wide?   _____ cm

B 20
1

33 _____
    7)18.06

34   5.72
       − 2.85
       _____

35   5.96
         3.85
       + 2.67
       _____

36   3.28
       ×   7
       _____

B3/B2
4

Circle the calculations that have a remainder of 4.

37–38 32 ÷ 7   33 ÷ 6   28 ÷ 8   31 ÷ 5

39–40 29 ÷ 3   76 ÷ 8   44 ÷ 5   41 ÷ 9

B 3
4

Double these values.

41 359   _____

42 £3.60   £ _____

B2/B3
2

43 Work out how many times you can subtract 28 from 476.   _____

44 A train leaves at 11:55 p.m. on Friday and arrives at 4:37 a.m. on Saturday. How long does the journey take?   _____ h _____ min

B3/B27
2

45 If £5.78 is shared equally among 17 people, how much does each person get?   £ _____

B 3
1

Halve these values.

46 £9.90   £ _____

47 $11\frac{1}{2}$ kg   _____ kg

B 3
B 10
2

My toolbox contains 2500 nails. $\frac{1}{4}$ are copper, 40% are zinc and the rest are bent.

48–50 I have _____ bent nails, _____ copper nails and _____ zinc nails.

B 10
B 12
3

Paper 17

Bodie drew a line graph to show the distance between himself and home on Tuesday.

B 14

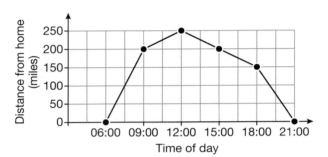

1 What was the furthest distance Bodie travelled from home?   _____ miles

2 How far from home was he at 3:00 p.m.?   _____ miles away

3–4 Between which two consecutive times did he travel the furthest? _____ and _____

5–6 Between _____ a.m. and _____ p.m. Bodie was 200 miles or more away from home.

7 What time did Bodie return home?   _____

8 Add all the even numbers between 9 and 21.   _____

B 2

9–10 A rectangle has a perimeter of 24 cm. It is half as wide as it is long.
   It is _____ cm long and _____ cm wide.

B 20

Rewrite these times for a 24-hour clock.

B 27

11 Half past 8 in the evening.   _____

12 Quarter past 12 in the morning.   _____

13 Quarter past 7 in the morning.   _____

14 How many 39p highlighters can be bought with £6.00?   _____

B3/B2

15 Subtract two hundred and eighty-eight from ten thousand.   _____

16 $30 \times 0.03 =$ _____

B 3

17 $60 \times 1.1 =$ _____

B 10

18 Add $\frac{1}{3}$ of 27 to twice 18.   _____

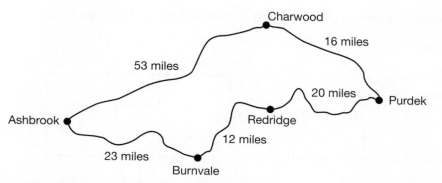

19 How far is it from Burnvale to Purdek via Redridge? _____ miles

20 What is the distance between Redridge and Charwood via Purdek? _____ miles

21 How long is the shortest route from Ashbrook to Purdek? _____ miles

22 What town is the furthest away by road from Burnvale? _____

23 There were 42 people at drama club. Eighteen left, but twice that number joined. How many are there now? _____

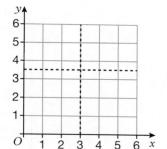

24 Plot and label the point A (2, 2).

25 Reflect this point in the vertical dashed line and label it B.

26 Reflect B in the horizontal dashed line and label it C. Join up A, B and C.

27 How many lines of symmetry does this shape have? _____

28 Which angle is a right angle: A, B or C? _____

29–31 This solid has _____ faces, _____ **vertices** and _____ edges.

49

32–34 Circle the three diagrams that are nets of the solid on the previous page.

B 21

a

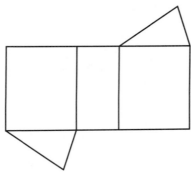

b

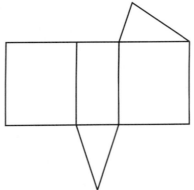

c

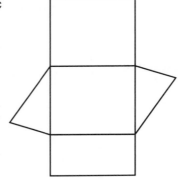

d

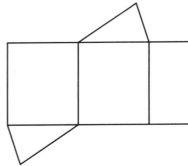

e

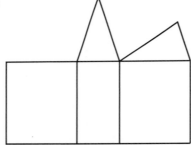

f

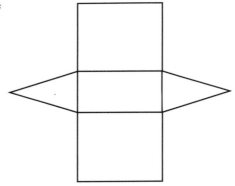

3

Complete these sequences.

35–36 $10\frac{1}{4}$ $10\frac{1}{2}$ $10\frac{3}{4}$ _____   _____

37–38 635   63.5   6.35   _____   _____

39–40 188   177   _____   _____

41   $\begin{array}{r} 6363 \\ + 1919 \\ \hline \end{array}$

42   $\begin{array}{r} 36 \\ \times 406 \\ \hline \end{array}$

43   $13\overline{)754}$ ____

44   $\begin{array}{r} 83.04 \\ 8.95 \\ + 4.08 \\ \hline \end{array}$

B 7
B 10
6
B2/B3
4

One-tenth of the cars in the car park are red. There are 30 cars altogether.

45 How many are not red? _____

B 10
1

There are 25 blank DVDs in a pack. Each pack of DVDs costs £1.99.

46 How many packs will you have to buy if you want 120 DVDs? _____

47 How much will you have to pay for 120 DVDs? £ _____

B 3
2

48 $435 \times 400 =$ _____

B 3
1

There were 110 people at a film. 38 left before the end.

49 How many watched the whole film? _____

B 2
1

50 Write the answer to this as a decimal.

$$8)\overline{309.6}$$

B 3
1

Now go to the Progress Chart to record your score!   Total   50

Paper 18

From this plan of a gym, calculate the areas used for each type of workout.

B 20

1 Weights = _____ m²

2 Bikes = _____ m²

3 Rowing machines = _____ m²

3

4–7 The pairs of **factors** of 14 are: _____ and _____, and _____ and _____.

8–13 The pairs of **factors** of 28 are: _____ and _____, _____ and _____, and _____ and _____.

B 5
10

Ravi completed 15 of his homework questions. Rochelle completed twice as many questions yet only managed to do half of the total questions.

14 How many questions did Rochelle complete? _____

15 How many questions were set for their homework? _____

B 3

2

B 5

B 3

For each of the questions, choose one number from each box.

16–17 Which numbers can be divided exactly by 5 and 3? _____ and _____

18–19 Which numbers have a remainder of 1 when divided by 4? _____ and _____

4

Write each of these fractions as a decimal.

20 $\frac{1}{5}$ _____

21 $\frac{7}{10}$ _____

22 $\frac{11}{100}$ _____

B 10

B 11

3

Write each of these decimals as a fraction in its **lowest term**.

23 0.03 _____

24 0.12 _____

B 11

2

25 7.109
  − 3.164
  _____

26 5.021
  × 3
  _____

27 _____
  7)1.309

B2/B3

3

28–31 Label the **acute angles** 'A', the **obtuse angles** 'O' and the **reflex angles** 'R'.

B 17

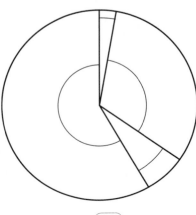

4

52

Match the calculations from list A with the ones from list B that have the same value.

List A	List B
26 × 3	105 − 98
80 − 14	3 × 29
12 + 75	156 ÷ 2
63 ÷ 9	6 × 11

32 _____ = _____

33 _____ = _____

34 _____ = _____

35 _____ = _____

36 If one book of stamps costs £3.60, how many books can you buy for £18.00? _____

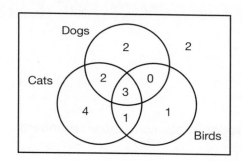

A vet has drawn this Venn diagram for all the pets owned by families living in his street.

37–38 _____ families own cats and _____ families own birds.

39 How many families live on the vet's street? _____

40 How many families own pets with four legs? _____

41 How many families do not have any pets? _____

42 A TV show started at 8:00 p.m. It lasted for 48 minutes and there were
9 minutes of advertising. When did the show finish? _____ p.m.

43 $6^2 + 2^2 =$ _____

44 $7^2 + 8^2 =$ _____

45 What is the square root of 81? _____

| £1 = 85 Indian rupees |
| £1 = 2 Singaporean dollars |
| £1 = 130 Sri Lankan rupees |
| £1 = 70 Thai baht |

46 How many Singaporean dollars can you get for £100? $ _____

47 How many Indian rupees can you get for £100?   _____ rupees

48 What are 650 Sri Lankan rupees worth in pounds?   £ _____

49 If you have 21 000 Thai baht, how many pounds can you get?   £ _____

50 Randall saves $\frac{3}{7}$ of his pocket money every week. If he saves £2.40 each time, how much does he spend?   £ _____

Now go to the Progress Chart to record your score!   **Total** 50

Paper 19

Complete these changes of **improper fractions** to **mixed numbers**.

1 $\frac{22}{10} = 2\frac{1}{}$ **2** $\frac{}{3} = 4\frac{1}{3}$

3 $6\frac{1}{7} = \frac{}{7}$ **4** $\frac{}{6} = 1\frac{2}{3}$

Write the correct sign, $<$, $>$ or $=$, in each space.

5 4×5 _____ $19 + 3$ **6** $9 - 7$ _____ $14 \div 7$

7 $12 \div 4$ _____ $3 - 1$ **8** $2 \times (3 + 10)$ _____ $3 \times (9 - 1)$

What fraction of the square is:

9 dotted?   _____

10 grey?   _____

11 dotted or grey?   _____

12 covered in crosses or dots?   _____

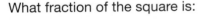

13–14 Two consecutive numbers multiply to 72. What are they? _____ and _____

B6/B3

15 What is the **range** in this set of numbers?

33   37   39   37   38

_____

B 15

16 A cake mix uses 4 cups of flour for every half-cup of cocoa.
How many cups of cake mix can I make with 1.5 cups of cocoa? _____ cups

B 3

17 What number is double 36? _____

B 3

18 I have £10. How much money would I have in New Zealand dollars? $ _____

| £1 = 2.867 Australian dollars |
| £1 = 3.22 New Zealand dollars |
| £1 = 17 120 Indonesian rupiahs |

B 3

19 How much is £10 in Australian dollars? $ _____

20 How much is £10 in Indonesian rupiahs? _____ rupiahs

21 How many rupiahs can I get for £35? _____ rupiahs

4

```
      11 cm        12 cm        13 cm        14 cm
   |||||||||||||||||||||||||||||||||||||||||||||||
           ↑      ↑           ↑      ↑      ↑
          Will    Ashanti    Kate   Angie  Dan
```

B 26
B 2

Some children measured the length of their feet with a ruler and wrote down the results.

22 How much longer is Dan's foot than Ashanti's? _____ cm

23 What is the difference between the longest and shortest feet? _____ cm

24 How much shorter is Will's foot than Kate's? _____ mm

25 What is the difference between Ashanti's foot and Angie's? _____ mm

4

Complete these fractions.

B 10

26 $\dfrac{}{5} = \dfrac{10}{25}$

27 $\dfrac{3}{10} = \dfrac{}{70}$

28 $\dfrac{}{6} = \dfrac{35}{42}$

29 $\dfrac{4}{11} = \dfrac{}{55}$

30 $\dfrac{}{9} = \dfrac{24}{54}$

31 $\dfrac{7}{9} = \dfrac{}{45}$

6

32 Write out 55 050 in words.

_____

B 1
1

33 What number gives an answer of 8 remainder 3 when it is divided by 9? _____ B 3

34–38 Complete this table. B 27

Buses leave at	Journey time	Buses arrive at
08:15	25 minutes	_____
_____	40 minutes	11:15
11:30	_____ minutes	11:57
12:45	35 minutes	_____
_____	45 minutes	14:30

39–40 The product of two numbers is 24. The difference between them is an odd number. The smaller number is _____ and the larger number is _____. B 5

41 A teacher has a packet of star-shaped stickers. Fifty per cent are gold, 25% are silver and 9 are bronze. How many stickers does she have altogether? _____ B 12

42 How far will a truck going at a constant speed of 50 km/h (50 km in 1 hour) travel in 90 minutes? _____ km B 3

Here is a line graph that shows the number of hours of sunshine in oneweek. B 14

B 2

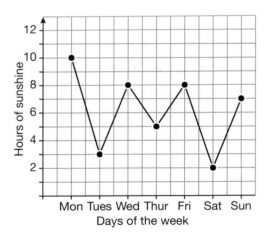

Days of the week

43 On how many days did the sun shine for more than 5 hours? _____

44–45 On which days did the sun shine for less than 4 hours? _____ and _____

46 How many hours of sunshine were there all week? _____ hours

47 How many hours of sunshine were there on Tuesday, Wednesday and Friday altogether? _____ hours

What is 2873 rounded to the nearest:

48 ten? _____

49 hundred? _____

50 thousand? _____

Now go to the Progress Chart to record your score! Total ◯ 50

Paper 20

1 What is the difference between 3300 and 33? _____

2 What number is halfway between 15 and 7? _____

3 If 3 times a number is 42, what is 4 times the number? _____

4 Jamal ate five-sixths of his Easter eggs in one day. If he has 3 left, how many did he start with? _____

What number does each symbol represent?

5 $(5 \times \square) \div 2 = 15$ $\square =$ _____

6 $(\triangle \div 3) + 4 = 8$ $\triangle =$ _____

7 $(12 - \blacksquare) \times 3 = 21$ $\blacksquare =$ _____

8 $(2 \times \diamond) - 5 = 21$ $\diamond =$ _____

E •

• B

•
C

•
D

A •

9 Join A to C. How long is the line? _____ mm

10 Join B to D. How long is the line? _____ mm

11 Join E to B. How long is the line? _____ mm

12 Is angle DBE **acute**, **reflex** or **obtuse**? _____

13   8010
   − 798
   _____

14   397
   × 20
   _____

Write in the missing numbers.

15 _____ m = 40 cm   **16** 0.6 km = _____ m   **17** _____ litres = 500 ml

18 526 mm = _____ cm   **19** 1.64 km = _____ m   **20** _____ kg = 1800 g

21–25 Complete this multiplication table.

×	3	_____	9
2	6	_____	18
_____	12	24	_____
9	_____	54	81

26 Rose thinks of a number, adds 3 then divides by 2. The answer is 29.
What is Rose's number?   _____

27 Jared can run round his school's 400 m track in 1 minute 4 seconds.
How long would 100 m take if he ran at the same speed?   _____ seconds

28 Gayle left home at 8:15 a.m. and arrived at school at 12 minutes to 9.
How long did she take?   _____ minutes

29–34 Complete the brackets in this multiplication table.

×	(____)	(____)	(____)
(____)	15	35	
(____)		49	77
(____)	27		99

Imran sees the following three clocks just as the train due at 10 past 11 arrives at the station.

Decide if the train was early or late according to each clock. Write the number of minutes and circle the correct word.

35–36 _____ minutes   early
                                        late

58

37–38 _____ minutes early / late

39–40 _____ minutes early / late

41–42 In a flowerbed there are 210 tulips. $\frac{3}{7}$ of them are red, $\frac{1}{7}$ are yellow and the rest are orange. There are _____ red tulips and _____ orange tulips.

Here is a line graph that shows the amount of water in my garden water butt at the end of each day.

43–44 On which days did it rain? _____ and _____

45 On which day did I use water from the water butt? _____

46 How much water did I use? _____ litres

47 What is the difference between the lowest and the highest level of water in the butt in the week? _____ litres

48 A farm has 600 sheep. 60% of these are adults.

How many lambs are there? _____

49 If 25 out of 30 cars passed their MOT tests, what fraction (in its **lowest term**) failed? _____

50 Work out how many times you can subtract 6 from 132. _____

Now go to the Progress Chart to record your score! **Total** _____ 50

Paper 21

Circle the true statements.

1 3.6 metres < 358 cm $\qquad$ $\frac{1}{2}$ litre = 500 ml

2 12 g > 0.01 kg $\qquad$ 45 minutes > $\frac{4}{5}$ hour

3 By how much is 4.6 greater than 0.7? $\qquad$

4 What is 13.1 minus 0.5? $\qquad$

5 Shari thinks of a number. If she adds 2 then divides by 3 the answer is 3. What is the number? $\qquad$

6–7 If you add Charlie's age to Lila's age it comes to 21 years. Lila is 3 years older than Charlie. Lila is $\qquad$ years old and Charlie is $\qquad$ years old.

8 The larger of two numbers is 19. The difference between them is 17. What is the smaller number? $\qquad$

9–14 Complete this table.

	Side	Perimeter	Area
Square 1	9 cm	_____ cm	_____ cm²
Square 2	_____ m	_____ m	49 m²
Square 3	_____ mm	24 mm	_____ mm²

15 How many 16 cm tall boxes can be stacked in a single column under a shelf 64 cm high? $\qquad$

16 What is the **mode** in this set of numbers?

17 11 13 15 18 18 11 9 7 11 12 11 14 $\qquad$

17 What is the **range** in this set of numbers? 13 8 12 15 $\qquad$

Circle the number that is equal to the fraction.

18 $\frac{21}{100}$ 2.1   2.01   0.021   0.21   21

19 $\frac{17}{50}$ 34   3.4   0.34   0.034   0.0034

20 $\frac{173}{100}$ 1.73   17.3   173   0.173   0.0173

A

B

C

21–29 Complete the table, saying whether the number is odd or even for each shape.

	A	B	C
Number of faces			
Number of **vertices**			
Number of edges			

Eric should start at work at 8:30 a.m. He was 16 minutes late on Monday.

30 What time did he actually start work? _____ a.m.

If he continues to be an extra 16 minutes late each day after that, at what time does he start work on:

31 Wednesday? _____ a.m   **32** Friday? _____ a.m

33 Subtract 38 mm from 12 cm. _____ cm

34 How many seconds are there in a quarter of an hour? _____

35 What is the sum of 7 litres, 329 ml and 12.5 litres? _____ litres

Put a decimal point in each of the following numbers so that the 5 has a value of 50.

36 56413 _____   **37** 13564 _____

38 45631 _____   **39** 31456 _____

B 10
B 11
3
B 21
9
B 27
B 27
3
B25/B2
1
B 27
1
B25/B2
1
B 27
4

I bought 8 pens for £5.52. I paid using a £10 note.

40 How much did each pen cost? _____ p

41 How much change did I get? £ _____

42 My brother is paid 20p for every 100 g of cans he recycles. Last month he collected 1.5 kg. How much money was he paid? £ _____

43–46 Plot and label the points A (3,0), B (5,3), C (3,6) and D (1,3). Join up the points.

47 How many **obtuse angles** does this shape have? _____

48–49 Draw the lines of diagonals on this shape.

50 Circle the point that lies on both diagonals.

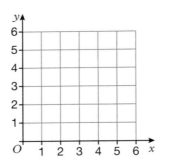

(0,0)   (4,3)   (2,4)   (3,3)   (5,3)

Now go to the Progress Chart to record your score! **Total** **50**

Paper 22

1 How many hours are there in 17 days? _____

2–4 Which numbers between 25 and 45 are exactly divisible by 7? _____ , _____ and _____

Complete these fractions.

5 $\frac{3}{10} = \frac{6}{\underline{}}$

6 $\frac{7}{7} = \frac{\overline{}}{9}$

7 $\frac{4}{8} = \frac{5}{\underline{}}$

8
$$\begin{array}{r} 1.83 \\ \times \quad 8 \\ \hline \end{array}$$

9
$$\begin{array}{r} 697 \\ \times \quad 21 \\ \hline \end{array}$$

10 _____ r ____
12)9128

Here is a table that shows the temperatures in different towns in Britain at midday and midnight on February 14th last year.

Town	Midday	Midnight
Moffat	3 °C	−6 °C
Swindon	5 °C	−1 °C
Lampeter	7 °C	4 °C
Liskeard	10 °C	−3 °C
Tonbridge	2 °C	3 °C

11 Where was the coldest place at midday? _____

12 What was the **range** of temperatures at midday? _____ °C

13 Where was the second coldest place at midnight? _____

14 Where was the biggest fall in temperature? _____

15–16 Which two places did not drop below freezing? _____ and _____

17 □○○△□○○△   What will the 13th symbol be? _____

18 ○◇△□○◇△□   What will the 12th symbol be? _____

19 ○○△□□○○△□□   What will the 17th symbol be? _____

Write each of these **improper fractions** as a **mixed number**.

20 $\frac{9}{4}$ = _____

21 $\frac{11}{8}$ = _____

22 $\frac{5}{4}$ = _____

23 $\frac{7}{2}$ = _____

24 $\frac{11}{6}$ = _____

25 $\frac{15}{3}$ = _____

26–27 A swimming pool has a perimeter of 78 m. If it is twice as long as it is wide, its length is _____ m and its width is _____ m.

Ishmael owns 9 grey mice, 3 white mice and 3 brown mice.

28 What fraction of the mice are brown? _____

29 What percentage of the mice are grey? _____ %

30 There are 36 children in Charlotte's class. $\frac{4}{9}$ of the class are boys. How many boys are there? _____

B 6

B 15

6

B 7

3

B 10

6

B 20

2

B 10

B 12

2

B 10

1

Place these decimals in descending order.

31–35 3.15   3.05   3.51   3.25   3.52

_____   _____   _____   _____   _____

Distances are in kilometres.

London				
328	**Manchester**			
1782	2126	**Oslo**		
420	764	1791	**Paris**	
1812	2156	2591	1418	**Rome**

36 Jean-Pierre is driving with his family from Paris to Rome.
How far is that? _____ km

37 Is it further from London to Oslo or from London to Rome? _____

38 What is the difference between these two distances? _____ km

39 How much further is it from Rome to Manchester than from
Paris to London? _____ km

Write each fraction as a decimal.

40 $\frac{33}{100}$ _____

41 $\frac{27}{50}$ _____

Remember: hens are adult female chickens. Cockerels are adult male chickens.

Arkvale Farm has 2224 chickens. There are 1108 adult birds and 1682 hens and chicks.

42 How many chicks are there? _____

43 How many hens are there? _____

44 How many cockerels are there? _____

45 The ages of Jean and Eloise add up to 26 years. Jean is 4 years older than Eloise,
so Eloise is _____ years old.

46–48 Which three consecutive numbers add up to 81? _____ , _____ and _____

A path is 2.5 m long and 1 m wide.

49 What is the area of this path? _____ m^2

50 What is the perimeter of this path? _____ m

B 11
5
B 14
B 2
4
B 10
B 11
2
B 2
3
B 2
1
B6/B2
B 3
3
B 20
2

Paper 23

Complete these number sequences.

B | 7

1–2   9   _____   15   18   21   24   _____

3–4   _____   29   23   _____   11

5–6   5   _____   10   12.5   15   _____

7–8   _____   99.9   9.99   0.999   _____

9–10   1   _____   9   16   25   _____

11 If 5 kilograms of cement cost £7.80, how much is $\frac{1}{4}$ kg?   £ _____

12 What number am I thinking of, if the remainder is 6 when 4 times the number is taken from 58?   _____

13 The sum of two numbers is 53. The larger number is 27. What is the other number?   _____

Look at this timetable.

	Bus 1	Bus 2	Bus 3
Kingslea	10:45	13:05	14:40
Queensmead	10:59	13:26	14:59
Netherton	11:16	13:47	15:16
Middleton	11:33	14:10	15:33
Overton	12:02	14:45	16:01

14 How long does the first bus take to travel from Kingslea to Overton?   _____ h _____ min

15 How long does the next bus take to do the same trip?   _____ h _____ min

16 Which of the three buses does this journey the fastest?   _____

17 How much longer does the second bus take to travel from Queensmead to Overton than the third bus?   _____ minutes

18   8.37
    − 4.48
    _____

19   16.29
    + 12.72
    _____

20   522
    × 7.2
    _____

21   _____
   23)7061

B10/B3   1
B2/B3   1
B | 2   1
B | 27
4
B2/B3   4

Islamabad is 5 hours ahead of London (+5 hours). Los Angeles is 8 hours behind London (−8 hours).

22 It is 2:00 p.m. in London. What time is it in Islamabad? _____

23 When it is noon in Los Angeles, what time is it in London? _____

24 When it is 7:30 p.m. in London, what time is it in Los Angeles? _____

25 What time is it in Islamabad when it is 5:30 a.m. in Los Angeles? _____

Round each of these numbers to the nearest 100.

26 48 126 _____

27 39 057 _____

28 29 292 _____

29 53 444 _____

30 89 089 _____

31 Three numbers are multiplied together to make 520. Two of the numbers are 13 and 10. What is the third number? _____

32 Add all the odd numbers between 12 and 24. _____

Here is a frequency table that shows the colours of cars that passed by Almond School in an hour.

Colour	Number of cars
Red	32
Yellow	15
Orange	8
Green	17
Blue	28

33 How many cars passed the school? _____

34 Which colour was seen the least? _____

35 How many more red cars were there than green? _____

36–37 Which two colours make up 40% of the cars? _____ and _____

38–46 Complete the table below for these solids.

A

B

C

	A	B	C
Number of faces			
Number of **vertices**			
Number of edges			

B 21

9

47 What is 93.3 divided by 300? _____

48 $0.3 \times 0.3 \times 0.1 =$ _____

49 What is 0.6 multiplied by 4.37? _____

B 11

3

50 There are 35 oranges in a box. If there is 1 lemon in the box for every 5 oranges, how many oranges and lemons are there altogether? _____

B 13

B 4

1

Now go to the Progress Chart to record your score!   Total 50

Paper 24

What are the next three terms in each of these number sequences?
Write fractions in the **lowest term**.

B7/B10

1–3	10	13	14	17	18	_____ _____ _____

4–6 $\frac{9}{10}$ $\frac{4}{5}$ $\frac{7}{10}$ _____ _____ _____

7–9 96   95   85   84   74   _____ _____ _____

10–12 0.1   0.3   0.5   _____ _____ _____

12

13 Write out 14 917 in words.

_____

B 1

14 A rectangle is 6.5 cm long and 2.98 cm wide. What is its perimeter? _____ cm

15 Subtract 96 centimetres from 4.8 metres. _____ m

B 20

B2/B25

3

Put a decimal point in each of the following numbers so that the 3 has a value of 3 tenths.

16 693 _____   **17** 369 _____   **18** 936 _____

19 963 _____   **20** 639 _____

21–26 Complete the brackets in this multiplication table.

×	(___)	(___)	(___)
(___)	20	40	
(___)		48	18
(___)	36		27

The local train takes 47 minutes to travel from Arkton to Biddlemere.

27 The 09:36 from Arkton arrives in Biddlemere at ___ : ___ .

28 The ___ : ___ from Arkton arrives in Biddlemere at 12:36.

29 Yesterday the train arrived in Biddlemere at 18:05. It was 11 minutes late.

What time did it leave Arkton?   ___ : ___

30 Janek spent half of his shopping money on bread, saved a quarter of it, and spent the rest on milk. If he spent £2 on milk, how much did he start with?   £ _____

31 Add $\frac{1}{6}$ of 18 to twice 17.   _____

32 Jonas has £45 in his bank account. He took out £9 and then put back three times as much as he took out. How much money does he have now?   £ _____

Write down the missing numbers.

33 5 × 8 × _____ = 400   **34** 4 × 5 × _____ = 1000   **35** 6 × 3 × _____ = 360

36 Work out how many times you can subtract 0.07 from 22.4.   _____

B 1

5

B 3

6

B27/B2

3

B10/B2

1

B10/B2

B 3

1

B2/B3

1

B 3

3

B2/B3

B 11

1

37
```
   101
    14
    47
 +  96
 _____
```

B 2
1

38 In a class, 18 girls have long hair and 3 girls have short hair.
What fraction (in the **lowest term**) of the girls have short hair?   _____

B 10
1

39 A bus left Kirkwall Church at 11:51 and took 13 minutes to get to
Stable Yard. When did it arrive?   _____ : _____

B 27
1

B26/B15

Here is a bar graph that shows the race times for a 70 m sprint.

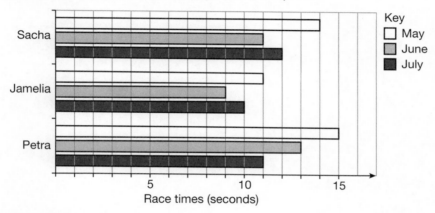

Key
☐ May
▨ June
■ July

Race times (seconds)

40 Who ran the slowest time?   _____

41 Who ran the fastest time?   _____

42 Who improved her time in every race?   _____

43 What is the **range** of the race times?   _____ seconds

44 What is the **mode** time for the 70 m sprint?   _____ seconds

45 Who won every race?   _____

6

B10/B12

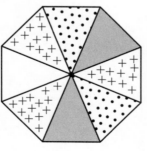

What fraction of the octagon (in **lowest terms**) is:

46 covered with crosses? _____

47 either grey or dotted? _____

48 What percentage of the octagon is grey? _____ %

49 What percentage of the octagon is not dotted? _____ %

50 How many more pieces would need to be dotted to cover 50% of
the octagon? _____

5

Now go to the Progress Chart to record your score!   Total   50

Progress Chart   Maths 9–10 years Book 2

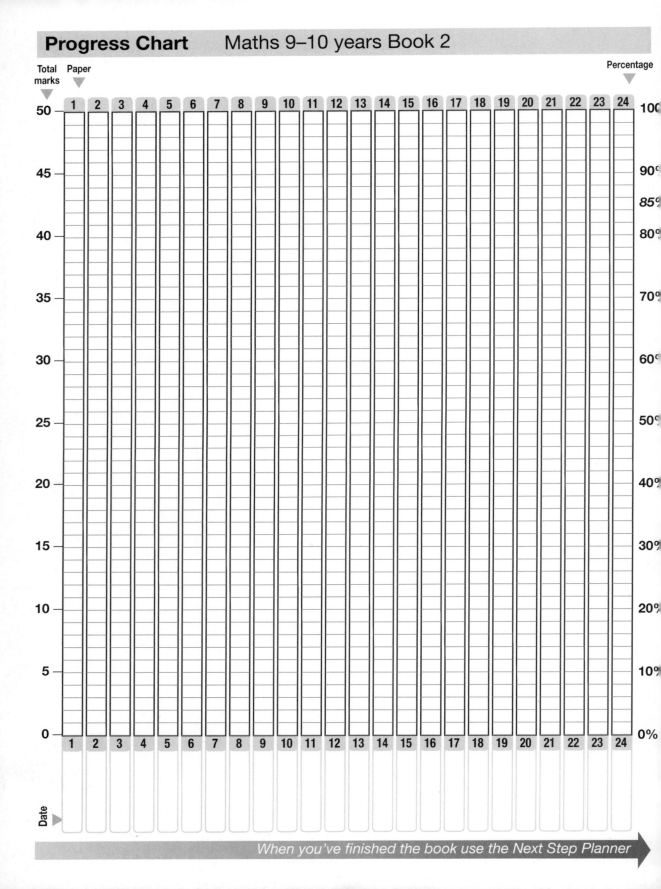

When you've finished the book use the Next Step Planner